An
Army
ABC Book

Written by: Kristen T. Pirog
Illustrated by: Julie A. Pierce

An Army ABC Book
is written by Kristen T. Pirog
illustrated by Julie A. Pierce
Copyright © 2010 Kristen T. Pirog and Julie A. Pierce

This is not an official US Army publication and the contents of this book are not endorsed by the US Government, Department of Defense, or Department of The Army.

Published and Printed by:
Steuben Press
an Imprint of R&R Graphics, Inc.
230 Primrose Court, Unit #1
Longmont, CO 80501

Printed in the United States of America

I.S.B.N. 978-0-9823131-5-2

KTP - To my Dad, retired Major David Turner,
who started me on this adventure,
and to my husband, Major John E. Pirog,
who continues to hold my hand and heart on that journey.

JAP - To my husband, CH(CPT) C. Christian Pierce
and to Joshua, Ellen, Ansley, and Emery

In memory of Major Douglas E. Sloan

A a
ALPHA

Airborne

B b

B R A V O

Boots

C c

CHARLIE

Chinook

D d
DELTA

Dog Tags

E e

E C H O

Eagle

F f
FOXTROT

Family

G g

GOLF

Guidon

H h

HOTEL

Humvee

I i

I N D I A

ID Card

J j

JULIETTE

Jump Wings

K k

KILO

K-9

L l

L I M A

Letters From Home

Your Family
Back Home
Fort Benning GA
31905

My Hero
3rd BDE 3rd ID
OIF III
APO AE 09397

nd Dad
Home
Illinois

Basic Trainee
Sand Hill
Fort Benning GA
31905

Our
101 Eagle
Fort Campbell KY
42223

M m
MIKE

Map

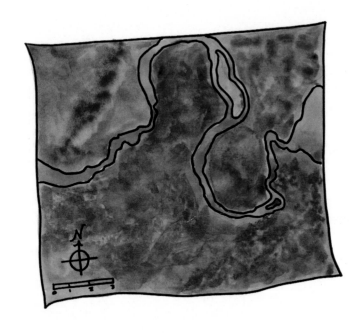

N n

NOVEMBER

New
Recruit

O o

OSCAR

Old Glory

P p
P A P A

Purple Heart

Q q
QUEBEC

Quarters

R r

ROMEO

Ranger

S s

SIERRA

Soldier

T t

TANGO

Tank

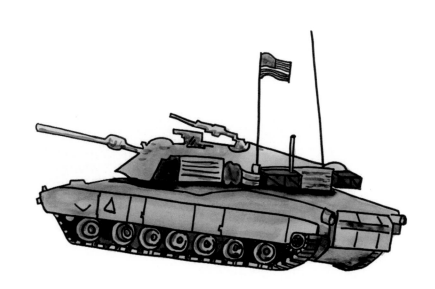

U u
UNIFORM

U.S.A.

V v

V I C T O R

Values

DUTY Loyalty

RESPECT

Selfless~Service

Honor

Integrity

Personal Courage

W w
WHISKEY

Worldwide

X x
X - R A Y

X-Ray

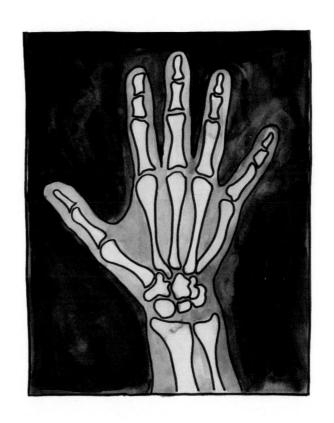

Y y
Y A N K E E

Yellow
Ribbon

Z z

ZULU

Zulu Time

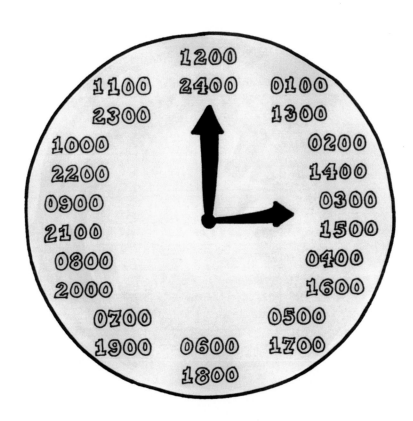

The Military Child

My hometown is nowhere,
My friends are everywhere.
I grew up with knowledge that home is where the heart is and the family is.
Mobility is my way of life.
Some wonder about roots, yet they are as deep and strong as the mighty oak.
I sink them quickly, absorbing all an area offers and hopefully giving enrichment in return.
Travel has taught me to be open.
Shaking hands with the universe,
I find brotherhood in all men.
Farewells are never easy.
Yet, even in sorrow comes strength and ability to face tomorrow with anticipation.
If when we leave one place, I feel that half my world is left behind,
I also know that the other half is waiting to be met.
Friendships are formed in hours and kept for decades.
I will never grow up with someone, but I will mature with many.
Be it inevitable that paths part, there is a constant hope that they will meet again.
Love of country, respect and pride fill my being when Old Glory passes in review.
When I stand to honor the flag, so also do I stand in honor of all soldiers,
And most especially, to the parents whose life created mine.
Because of this, I have shared in the rich heritage of **Military** life.

Anonymous

About the Authors

Kristen T. Pirog is an Army Brat and Army wife.
She is a former middle school teacher who currently lives in Texas
with her husband John and their two little Army Brats Ellie and Molly.

Julie A. Pierce is an artist and Army wife.
She is a former middle school art teacher who currently lives in Georgia
with her husband Christian and their four children
Joshua, Ellen, Ansley, and Emery.

An Army ABC Book

by **Kristen T. Pirog**
and **Julie A. Pierce**

I.S.B.N. 978-0-9823131-5-2

Order Online at:
www.SteubenPress.com

By Phone at:
303-482-2060

A portion of the proceeds from this book will go to Army charities,
including Operation Remembrance, which provides
keepsake boxes to the families of fallen soldiers.
For more information, email: admin@operationremembrance.org
or go to: www.operationremembrance.org